Pebble® Plus

Aircraft

Hang Gliders

by Mari Schuh

Consulting Editor: Gail Saunders-Smith, PhD

Consultant: Stewart W. Bailey, Curator
Evergreen Aviation & Space Museum
McMinnville, Oregon

CAPSTONE PRESS
a capstone imprint

Pebble Plus is published by Capstone Press,
1710 Roe Crest Drive, North Mankato, Minnesota 56003
www.capstonepub.com

Library of Congress Cataloging-in-Publication Data
Schuh, Mari C., 1975–
  Hang gliders / by Mari Schuh.
    p. cm.—(Pebble plus. Aircraft)
  Includes bibliographical references and index.
  ISBN 978-1-62065-112-4 (library binding)
  ISBN 978-1-4765-1068-2 (eBook PDF)
1. Hang gliding—Juvenile literature. I. Title.
GV764.S37 2013
797.5′5—dc23   2012029196

Editorial Credits
Erika L. Shores, editor; Heidi Thompson, designer; Eric Manske, production specialist

Photo Credits
Corbis: Kevin Fleming, 15; Dreamstime: Aleksandra Lande, 13, Elena Koulik, 9, Marlene Cabais, 7, Neale Cousland, 5, Pniesen, 19; National Geographic Stock: Skip Brown, 17; Newscom: Pollicv Flight Collection, 11; Shutterstock: Alexandra Lande, cover, Andrea Catenaro, 21

Artistic Effects
Shutterstock: New Line

The author dedicates this book to Ben Krizek of Racine, Wisconsin.

Note to Parents and Teachers

The Aircraft set supports national science standards related to science, technology, and society. This book describes and illustrates hang gliders. The images support early readers in understanding the text. The repetition of words and phrases helps early readers learn new words. This book also introduces early readers to subject-specific vocabulary words, which are defined in the Glossary section. Early readers may need assistance to read some words and to use the Table of Contents, Glossary, Read More, Internet Sites, and Index sections of the book.

Printed in China
092012   006934LEOS13

Table of Contents

Hang Gliders

What's that up in the sky?
Hang gliders look
like big kites.
These simple flying machines
glide through the air.

Parts of Hang Gliders

Hang gliders have strong frames made of light metal tubes. Many hang gliders weigh less than 80 pounds (36 kilograms).

The frame looks like
a triangle-shaped wing.
Strong nylon fabric
covers the frame.

Pilots hang from a harness

under the wing.

A helmet protects

the pilot's head.

Flying a Glider

To fly a hang glider,

pilots face the wind.

Then they run down

a hill or off a cliff.

Pilots steer by moving their weight from side to side. They hold onto a bar to help them steer.

A boat or small airplane
helps some hang gliders fly.
The boat or airplane pulls
the glider until it's moving
fast enough to fly.

Hang gliding is a fun sport.

Gliders can travel up to 100 miles

(160 kilometers) in one flight.

Air flowing over the wing keeps

the glider up in the air.

Up, Up, and Away!

How far will it glide?

A hang glider lets

a person soar like a bird.

Glossary

cliff—a high, steep wall of rock or earth

frame—the main part of a hang glider over which fabric is stretched; frames are made of light metal such as aluminum or graphite

glide—to move smoothly and easily

harness—straps and fabric that safely hold a pilot while flying

nylon—a very strong material that is used to make cloth

steer—to move in a certain direction

Read More

Hicks, Kelli L. *Hang Gliding and Paragliding.* Action Sports. Vero Beach, Fla.: Rourke Pub., 2010.

Kelley, K. C. *Hang Gliding.* Mankato, Minn.: Child's World, 2011.

Meredith, Susan. *How Do Aircraft Fly?* Science in the Real World. New York: Chelsea Clubhouse, 2010.

Internet Sites

FactHound offers a safe, fun way to find Internet sites related to this book. All of the sites on FactHound have been researched by our staff.

Here's all you do:

Visit *www.facthound.com*

Type in this code: 9781620651124

Super-cool stuff! Check out projects, games and lots more at **www.capstonekids.com**

23

Index

Word Count: 174
Grade: 1
Early-Intervention Level: 18